Red Channel in the Rupture

RED CHANNEL
IN THE RUPTURE

Poems

Amber Flora Thomas

Red Hen Press | *Pasadena, CA*

Book layout by Amber Lucido

Library of Congress Cataloging-in-Publication Data
Names: Thomas, Amber Flora, author.
Title: Red channel in the rupture : poems / Amber Flora Thomas.
Description: First edition. | Pasadena, CA : Red Hen Press, [2018]
Identifiers: LCCN 2018031080 | ISBN 9781597096195 (tradepaper)
Classification: LCC PS3620.H6246 A6 2018 | DDC 811/.6—dc23
LC record available at https://lccn.loc.gov/2018031080

The National Endowment for the Arts, the Los Angeles County Arts Commission, the Ahmanson Foundation, the Dwight Stuart Youth Fund, the Max Factor Family Foundation, the Pasadena Tournament of Roses Foundation, the Pasadena Arts & Culture Commission and the City of Pasadena Cultural Affairs Division, the City of Los Angeles Department of Cultural Affairs, the Audrey & Sydney Irmas Charitable Foundation, the Kinder Morgan Foundation, the Meta & George Rosenberg Foundation, the Allergan Foundation, the Riordan Foundation, and the Amazon Literary Partnership partially support Red Hen Press.

First Edition
Published by Red Hen Press
www.redhen.org

Acknowledgments

I wish to thank the following publications where some of these poems first appeared:

Alaska Quarterly Review, "Rattlesnake"; *Callaloo*, "The Moon That Night," "Shed," "Twenty Days and Another Bat"; *Connotation Press: An Online Artifact*, "A Wild Thing," "The Age of Forgetting," and "The Old Horse"; *Ecotone*, "How to Leave Her," "Moment in Which Self Moves Under Song"; *New England Review*, "Manifesto at the Well," "Orchid"; *Poem-a-Day*, "Damaged Photos," "Headwind"; *Saranac Review*, "Passing," "Pollen"; *Spillway Magazine*, "Atlantic," "Crown Vetch," "Horse Head, Navarro Beach"; *Third Coast Magazine*, "Self-Portrait with Teeth"; and *Tin House Magazine*, "Cupid."

Also, I would like to thank my Cave Canem Foundation family of fellows, faculty, and staff for holding me in the light of poetry with acceptance, love, and truth. I am braver and my joy more boundless after knowing your voices and poems. Your names are too numerous to list here, but Toi Derricotte and Cornelius Eady: thank you for knowing what was needed and making the circle possible.

Contents

I. Stills

II. Apertures

III. Reels

"I can only distinguish
one thread within running hours
you   flowing through selves
toward You."

—Audre Lorde

Red Channel in the Rupture

I.

Stills

Damaged Photos

You get into puddles with the sky
and when this fails
pit your girl against an ocean.

Choices blur and make off with rooms
in the whiteness. Winged enough to manage
your red kimono's thirty-seven cranes in various
trajectories while you make the coffee.

You as God with rattlesnakes
and His Admiral Death holding down the muscle,
headless and breath swollen.

You scattered in her facelessness
behind the screen door, not frowning, not joyous,
just working her hands in a dish towel,
folding them away.

You as ether, over-exposed bursting place,
dulling with these selves, spun by light
and dropped into shadow places,
forgotten as you put the photos down.

An Opening

This morning the raiment
of a dead bat stops me
on the sidewalk, outside an abandoned
house on Main Street, and I find

my attention slipped
into narrow chambers
where a tutelage of insects

escapes. I stop,
though for clear horrors,
teeth cracked and ears

crushed to fish-scale, sun-rich
flaking. A brace too brittle
for thimble or spoon.

Velvet tufts gather in
my gaze and pocket
the lightness just the same.

Where waters diminished
to sand in the wing's scuffing,
have closed, red unwoven

and stilled in ruptured channels,
sends salt as crystal
dust across my palm.

Parent shadows
fly out from the attic.
Poor bat, struck by the earth.

The Age of Forgetting

This happens with the rapture too.
Leaving your Birkenstocks and
brown sweater waiting at the chair
with a cold cup of coffee. A gift
of peacock feathers nodding in
a jar by the window. Served up

by science as brain atrophy. Shrapnel
misting cranial stars. Arias in oblivion
sending you into a remote outback
of lippy frostings and creams smeared
on spoons. Tripping until you tripped
into the white rabbit's belly fluff.

The rooms sucked away like cellophane
caramels and fizzy root beer pop. At first,
Great-great-grandmother Wickliffe and
our Cherokee in Tennessee appeared
as snapshots. Your newspaper route
in 1955. The stories you had to deny

undressed by cloud front. Your
disappearance like motion trapped
in a marble; the finite air bubbles
cruising that cosmos probably
breath. Little god raising your drunk,
smoked-out white flag at my entire life.

Moment in Which the Self Moves Under Song

I drew into me
a salt and bitter tongue that crested
and soaked the numb ladder through my limbs

and let you climb in,
rung after rung. I meant to breathe,
but I swallowed. And a world

that was spirit sang out.
A redwood eased her claw
on the window. I quivered.

Pulled off my knees, to slip outside the inlet,
where a foghorn groaned like an old cow
used to what was tearing through her.

Then fishing boats returning
to Noyo Harbor ahead of a fog bank
motored in, gulls' erratic circles

twisting after each boat, saviors
in mast lines screeching for castoffs.
Across docks, passages filled

with men, ice chests, and netting.
A dog trotted through the parking lot.
Neon signs woke with blinking.

The quick agreement between tire
and metal grating on the bridge
above the harbor clipped and roared

toward town. Laughter and yelling
below. Light through cypress gaps
stung rooftops across the way.

A thrumming in my throat. Why can't I get
to the door? The numb ladder through
my knees shook, and I tried

not to be a child for the last time.
The gulls soared. Heavy ropes knotted
around anchors strained. I choked

like a girl finished crying, mascara
and eyeshadow running from her gaze. I told her:
You are flesh, now bow. Uncross your legs.

Your curve is   open   bounty   pleasure.
I kept my eyes closed.
Boats gulped against the docks.

The redwood drew her craggy notes
on the window through the fog.
I climbed her branches out.

I made my mouth pretend
to be seaworthy while the waves
washed in. I could not angle

myself into any further distance.
I stood outside and watched the moon
put her shadows away

He Breaks in the Glare

The dark-eyed junco enters
                    the part of his existence
      which is all bone and
         quill decisions crushed
into splinters;
       yarn washed against brick.

The region of glass, false or not,
                blows out his skull,
     narrows and redefines
     a hemisphere
no song might know
     again.

At the High Bay Building, note
               the steady glare
in which the junco's final self
     is acquired. All along the west face,
various decrees with earth
     rot out in the rain.

Some weeks, maintenance
              drives a hand-broom along the wall
and the juncos put aside their joints
     to crumble against the broom's teeth.
This afternoon's bird makes
     a paperweight for fluttering propaganda:
     amazing   a maze a zing.

The warm song crushed back into lungs
                    when the junco couldn't pass through
        glass trained to be creaseless sky.
            His unfinished litany
        must be thirst
            pressing his tongue out to the rain.

Lizard and Moth

He breathed   black moth wings
        and they fought,
        head in the throat,
        neck skin ballooned.   Stealing

along the bark of a longleaf pine,   the fire fluttered
        and beat hard to leave
        the breast.

The flame was velvet
        and grew with night things,
        pulled into deep furrows,   scraggy plates,
        making flight   a crawler again.

Yellow-striped tail   curling on the bark
        as the front legs lifted—
        moments when   neither lizard nor moth
        won.

Reappeared   as a roaring:
        bullet in the leaves,
        shadow skipping a rock,
        coiling in a dream.   The lizard dragged

the moth to his scaly domain,

a dragon's bouquet   in circumference,
        drank night
        from the muse's red mouth,
        was   singing.

The Old Horse

He broke on linoleum flats
where he was made to play cowgirl.
Barrels and plastic cows he vaulted through
tumbled. His quarter split like a wing into the flank,
and his tail came away as well. Hollowness
all through the hoof.

The girl put her finger in the hole,
nicking her skin on a new edge, and thought
the horse trembled.

Leaning him against the barn, his three-legged
slouch facing a light pool in the hallway, she carried
his leg to her mother. "Fix this," she said.

Superglue later and his canter
tore through the blazing desert outside
the fence. Splinters showing,
the buff barrel racer stretched his neck
beneath her hand.

Always there then: her breath
trapped inside his body, that thin
pocket. The fragrant taste of plastics
and the mercury of loving him
so much, she could afford
to close away the song.

Rattlesnake

Too much mouth, too much
gasping outward with teeth
of white cords stuck in warning.
The shovel you force into

the retreating neck sparks
on rock: the tooth of one enters
the other in your removal
of the head. The coil loosens,

infinite then slack S.
The rock lips shade and
you reach in there for
the body; the diamondback

loops your forearm, a gaping
red and white, a forsaken effort
to teach you, and banished
from another day.

Bring me a Friday. Bring me
your death so I may tire
in the shadow with inevitable
litany; this memory again:

you hold out the helix
for me to draw a finger
along cool smooth skin,
and the throat answers, life again.

Rooted

If the beetle's black slips into iridescence
If the splinter and raft merge
If summer waste turns to awe
If against the weathered wood you write her name
If dappling etches through
If heather rusts in the drinking trough
If you look back
If she looks back
and the wing begins as a shell
and the rope spells between the rocks
If you drop the seed in and an oak climbs out
who then gathers
when you turn your singing away?
when you ball your socks in your boots
and wade out to the gods (minnows, all)
what about your narrow hours then?
when you've waited for the shell
to shake loose your wings?

Like Sun Slips Along the Vane

He is gone.
Praise the only feather found on a path.

Gone like tulips peeled by March.
Gone as a cardinal fleeing his own red split.

Not held from valley or mountain.
Not returned by the asphalt's north and south.

In your sleepiness, you say, "He is gone."
Days do not begin in his company.

Sweats and treats, "Baby,
good morning." Gone.

The mail arrives.
The cat scratches at the door.

You bury flat faces in a sink of soapy water,
scrubbing all that sourness gone.

Gone Crook.
Gone Foul Shoe.

He washes like a lament for an old fool.
Irish Springs' clean emerald gone.

His shortest sermon tacked to the wall.
Open the doors. Beat the rugs on a porch railing.

Call dibs on the old armchair.
Hallelujah. He is gone.

Passing

I am told I asked my father to stay
home, him being certainly black.
My prayers ate a complicated trail
into white-ist bargains. Assassinations

begin at home. Even Peter Rabbit
undressed for the farmer's cache.
"Ashes to ashes," my mother said.
Blackness rushed after me like

a heavy cloud. He read me passages
from the *I Ching*: "Mountains standing
close together keep still." He attempted
rescue with "colored," pushing the canon

across the lake when I tired of swimming.
An atrophy from fear being good: the inexact
home I exploited in my early chapters
only to be pleased with the storm.

He stood in the classroom doorway
and said my name three times
before I let myself see his brown face.
I let blackness ripple and then

I went to him, gunned through rows
by spitting bees. Eyes in horror
dashed me to rocks. But, I went to him.

Headwind

Weak motion of grasses and tern before the sea.
Worry's school cresting here and everywhere
as failings.

I pace the cliff path, my hands cupped above my eyes.
The glare steals your progress, a kayak needling
the wide open.

Love means you answer, this the child's rebuke.
A pattern crosses the point, hemming
the horizon: steamship.

I didn't know you were the green pitch
unable to beat the storm to shore.
You didn't know I was the lookout.

Get accustomed to the sad girl picking you
out of the sea, the knot caught in her throat,
and the unraveling of her speech: an endless rope
thrown out of me.

Feathering

Late morning and hot
on the Sound, you ask me
to watch your paddles execute
a feather angle. "It's easy,"
you say. "The wrist twists the blade
for the least resistance."

Our kayaks drift farther
apart, as I bring my paddles
too high, cutting an angle *into*
resistance, flat side dragging
and not slicing air. You follow me
and watch my technique.

In the river's center,
I haven't learned: muck
and depth churned by rough
current. The feather *is* opposition,
carrying otherwise doomed stones
through air. I quit, knowing

the byway one kayak opens
for the another, and I follow you
out further, fish throwing themselves
around us, silver splinters
like applause.

Shed

She is not afraid of gods. She leaves her skin,
still coiled, a great throat collapsed.
Gods have entered and left.

The door sounds like a throat clearing
in its rusty evolution toward shadow,
an atrium from scalding noon.

She treats the dark like a cathedral.
She is all swallow, the heart working
under every scale to outgrow a fortified spiral.

The cathedral swallows the heart.
Take up your broom. No gods are left.
She finished the mice in time for autumn's gloom.

There are some cathedrals like this shed
behind the house where she shunned her body
and in the dark was not afraid of gods.

Sunlight pushes past our legs
on the plywood and pools in the coiled skin
that overwintered.

Dig your broom into corners.
She is not afraid of gods or matriarchs.

Matrix

Here the fossil begins
in melodious shift of tide
to gather cement, a sediment

of mollusk, barnacle,
and other creature-clingers
in this hard-packed universe,

a skeletal dissemination
on the sea floor passing
for petrified finality.

House for eons put to rest,
fixed and loyal to the dolphin
who once swam to the air and

set its leaping across
the waves. Lord laid down,
pulled toward collusion,

giving us fin gods, shell gods,
microbial accumulation of gods
and their fossils being

the only place of remembrance.
Pocked chambers through
and striates combed

to the convex etched in, survives
starved of autonomy. The mass
takes the shape of what

you cannot make out.
And when asked say, "Yes,
I can see the dolphin in the stone."

Entry

A day like this, you hate the dog
and the other dog, even the field
where the cat hunkers down in purple heather
to spring on a dragonfly . . .
and the cat, too.

The leaning barn and the lover
who owns the pelt of a grizzly
draped on the couch
and burns your breakfast in a garlic sauce.

The plane putting a seam
in dawn's rusty start, a retreat
chased by eastward gusts.

Your worry holding off an ache
that sidles the grove
to spit out five jays.

You hate the ficus, its five-pointed palms
narrowing inward, as you pet
the lump and hue.

You've hushed and balled
a nattering groan
and woken still with love
cutting eyes at dawn.

Ending in Place

So good to meet the guard
looking east: cypress limbs
eclipsed by moss defend
angles in the wind.

Cattails rattle dry stocks,
thrumming beneath, all
the poised seeds shedding
death. A riot turns into applause.

A motorboat speeds
in the cleft between sandbars
up river, a spire dipping
a Confederate flag at the stern.

A bass feeds on sand
at your feet, wide-mouth
swallowing tidal wake.
Where the marsh spreads

reedy-toothed into forest,
a crab trap rots at the surface.
This, the thirteenth moon washes
your wandering, so you stand

in silt and weed on the path,
overturn a red bottle cap
to watch a translucent sprite
unbury itself.

Salt bears you into every song.
You could have run farther.
You could have been less loud.
But you are here. Be at home.

II.

Apertures

Neighborhood Boys

I climb out of every song
the mockingbird tries, to watch
an evening battle with pinecones. Neighborhood boys
twist and duck between needled grenades.

Scuttles across the pavement, cars
crushing the mess, which will wait
for the street sweeper on Tuesday.
Jubilant miss. Lucky cover.

Inevitable pout for a nicked ear. Arcing
hits, cleaving open the pincushion
of a bleed, and farther down
the bruise begins. Getting even

and getting good with their aim.
Jeans tugged up every third step.
Noses rubbed inside elbows. *Ha-ha*. Wasted
and sore until my yard is cleared.

The middle school boys
who traded marbles at recess
returning just now with the bargain
my five-year-old self took

because they were willing
to lose a blue wave
inside a clear sphere if I followed them
into the woods. The glass beaded

by a half-moon of air bubbles
no one had breathed in decades; finite source
teaching me it was possible to get stuck
anywhere. I traded the marble away

or lost it because I couldn't remember
the girl stepping out of the woods,
the bird in her turning its ruddy shoulder
toward the light, thankful she got to live,

that while they tried to kill her,
they could in the end let her live . . .
and on this street
where boys war with pinecones;

somehow, I owe them my life.

The Moon That Night

Having eaten your head clean off, my cat
drops your plump carcass on the doormat.
Between blood and purple clots, a bit of neck bone
insists on the air. I lean toward the sharpness,
get right up to the vacant white nipple, like milk
that has contested its cream and been deemed "fat-free."

Transparent like a baby's fingernail, the broken column
spills dead nerves. My cat licks her paw and smack!
your pudgy mass jumps, blood escaping into jute threads.

White like the full moon that night I was twelve
and we snuck up the road. He opened his blue jeans
and thrust his blunt eye at me. It was this
or nothing, he said. I wish I'd chosen nothing.
Later, the moon split the road with redwoods
and I relented to my home. Exhausted,
I didn't swing my arms at the bat stealing moths
above my head.

I didn't wake again until you, little mouse
resting in the middle of "welcome," until my cat
in whose wide green eyes I see myself
leaning from the doorway, and I remember.

Self-Portrait with Migraine

I was able to move toward morning
in un-weaned light across the lawn,
creatures walking to me chirped and wagged,
schoolchildren's forgotten shadows spread
into my reach, returning thin with laughter
to my mug of chamomile tea.

There had been nothing
but pain for days, eye-shutting,
bearing down on lightening, an endless
recess where the high whine of the merry-go-round
spun with the running push a child tucked into its rails,
tetherball flattening chain on the pole, unwinding again.

I was the stone dropped in four-square and the suck of the rope
drawing a blurry hemisphere around a girl in a plaid jumper.
Then the light was not so bad. I could open my eyes
and begin something, anything. Monday.
The wind played tag and scuttle in
the trees. Silence where there
had been hammering.

When You Are Hollow

Force in the wings,
tethered to a charity, rushing up
to swallow wind gusts
with a leafy orange tail.

The tongue seizes and flaps,
the kite spinning toward black
cliffs. Only the child's arms visible
in the field, tightening string

in time to send the dragon sailing
across the sun. It tames the torrent
with its mouth open, so air tears
through the torso. A lot of talk

with this string: joy, unhindered
by belief, roars in the succor of nylon
for however long he manages
the suck of wind.

And who will the child be
when the kite goes into the sea?
His arms threaded over
by snapped string, the bragging

runnel of a beast who must
answer to pleasure, deflated, nose
cracked and wings crisscrossed
against the churning shore.

Cupid

His wings rest at his feet.
His fists curl inside a brown paper bag.
The alert beak propped on his head

aims down the block into sidewalk pools
of streetlight. His red lips make plump
numbers. He has so much candy

the bottom bulges. A pumpkin arrives
on spindly orange legs, followed by
a skeleton crew of two with unkept

postures, baggy knees, and flaccid spines.
A ghost sidles up, his sheet belted,
a baseball cap holding sloppy eye holes

in place. He hurries off with his posse
of short immortals, leaving the
wings where he stood.

The mother says, "Oh, look,"
disappointment as she brushes rubble
from feathers. She searches through streetlight

for her angel, holding the wings
so he'll dig his arms through the straps,
shrugging on tonight's beast.

Pollen

after D. H. Lawrence

As a person come through,
I say "I." In a halo of sun-stung colonizers,
minions with this one chance to claim a forest,
I lift my hand. Among soldiers,

my sweater is static and my upturned
palm a worship. Is this the door
and the knocking I must yield

myself to? Rain puddles collect
a glassy sage soup. I sneeze
and sneeze, but inside I know the offer is valid.

The neighbors call, "Friday, here boy.
Friday come." The cheer of dog tags
ignites from the bushes.

I need a great story today.
Tell me, do you still want ten children
and a musical number that will sell out the house?

I've scattered in every direction
so you cannot breathe me in.
I will not be breathed in by you.

Cadence

The pressure of continental plates crushing
along the Hayward Fault ran a jagged contusion through her yard
and under a fence for miles north and south. She hopped

over the artery, sun linen in her skirt.
Weeds reached across the gap, tangled white-bud
and arrow in a scraggy bridge. This friend

who would steal the name I was saving
for my daughter (a daughter I didn't have anyway.)
Her a's and e's tasted over tea at the kitchen table.

Our spoons laden with honey and dunked in warm mugs,
while a vase of calla lilies centered before us
spilled a roiling ant parade on the tablecloth. I asked her

did she ever put her arm in the break, seismic vibration
just off the Pacific drawn into her bones,
humming around her heart.

I was low with ruptures I'd lived through,
regions of tear and ache, worried; I was always leaving.
She smiled.

I smiled.
All she wanted was a child. We spoke of this
into a second hour. *Ting. Ting.* Our spoons touched the insides of our mugs.

She gathered her skirt around her thighs to make the leap
across the broken world she owned.
She could have your name, your loss

when losing such a person was possible.
Little songs she'd put you out in the yard to sing
with peanut butter and banana. Verses you'd forget.

Sticky fingers held at your mouth. Sunlight looking at you
parceled by branches. You'd splinter and skip.
(Ruptures are all the same: unsettling.)
Your name to her own sweet root.

Orchid

Down in the holy
and maiden where
the singing is,
where you drink
and cup the rain
and cling to an
everglade mound.

The narrow throng
where amethyst deepens
into black, a place
waiting in the animal night
to be scooped up
or left alone—

the frill labellum. The shroud
where the shoot births
unfurling tongues
that couldn't hide their waves
when I brought you
to the nursery.

All around you a light
that put the pearl in there
and kneaded it like a pit
some girl could spit
into her palm.

Why I Go Back

To dive into breath
trapped by rolling green
air. To force my limbs open
and ring my tongue

in there, ready for praise
and the accolades of time
to free myself.

To unglue my spine
from shallows and tear myself
further down into silence,

so I can rise
from the deepest pool
among no others.

I towel off,
bent into pouring gaze
and stippled chill.

It is morning
and I've stopped
along Navarro River.

The past entered
here again,
so I dive.

Crossing

Defuse creature shaken by winter
heaves cold off the Sound,
long knuckles dragging Spanish moss
on every gust through the pines.

Heady rasping of maples
marking the path with browns and reds,
where a snake has been easily hid.

Soft cover sheltering all manner
of sleep: looked upon
with disruption.

Subtle waves peel at the shore.
Answers pour in, unfazed by winter's
approach in the upright groaning.

Space for each of them
that listen together. Most have left
when the snake comes upon them

as night crossing into the pines;
the path reaches the water where
the shore is brought high in
the flat gazes of summer homes.

Horse Head, Navarro Beach

Buried just up from shore,
a midnight, high-tide deposit.
My sister bends her shadow
over the mask and brings

both of us into seeing the
box jaw and narrow face in
what we thought a cypress
limb washed into hard pack.

Doesn't fit under my arm,
so I carry it against my sweater,
salt water and silt leaking from
smooth hollows. A triumphant

escape from the underworld.
Yet, no spine, flared mane,
or thick quarters follow. I burrow
two fingers in the nasal break,

dredging red clay and sand.
My sister rises and brushes
her palms on her jeans; no great
rumbling chariot today.

Seasons of creaking knots
and clatter in prize gear
forgotten, as I carry it out
across the dunes.

How to Leave Her

As a beautiful cut in
the frantic school of light,
crouching on the grey rocks
above the trail. Her temple self,
hissing. As a forgetting when
the mountain lion is gone
in three exact leaps.

As my running the sun down,
seven miles from roads and homes,
her tongue's needle under every rib.
A leg cramp through my fear
when I stop to press a knuckle
in the knot. The sun and dust and I
catching up.

As a change inside, not dying.
A report I will keep from rangers
and neighbors her beautiful cut
lost on the rocks above the trail.
I am changed by her not dying.
The two of us in one story now.

Down in the River

I went to church among those zeros,
kissed and tasted by pinheads,
each pucker of unashamed feasting
against my ankle skin.

Minnows scattering right
and left as I stepped better
into the estuary, flowed
as current to my legs,

inviting me into deeper pools,
pocked valleys of sand
and algae bloom.

Here was the sound: hushed
cords twisting muscle and flex
while they held themselves
against the shore of my being
there. And when I spoke,

I thought you would
damn the words in me,
only there was scattering
and return. Forgiveness,
finally.

Twenty Days and Another Bat

Tonight a solitary bat
lay wings open in the hallway.
I use a towel to scoop him
into my most gentle grip
and return him to the outside.

The porch door snaps behind us.
I set him on the wide wood stairs,
his zenith of terrors flops and flops
to the right.

Brethren screeching the stars down.
Yet, he won't fly. I step back
into the porch light's humming circle.
The whole wilderness was schooled to me as a girl,
but I have to step away.

Humid dark promises
an early morning rain. Sweat trickles
along my neck. "Go little horror," I say.
"The matron will bust your back
with her broom."

Fine velvet smarts turn an awful hiss,
a banishment of our presence
in the light, denouncements
that reverberate through me.

Then his splintering flight
as he enters all the triumphant shrills of night
where blindness is not a sham.

Atlantic

My dog chases a sandpiper
toward the surf, chasing, chasing
until the bird flies off, both of them
snagged by a wave's foamy edge.

A crescent washes my boot.
New moons everywhere I turn.
Growling and purring, sand releases
the wave and tigers retreat.

My dog looks at me, looks at where
the sandpiper flew, brow furrowed
and ears up. Is this joy? The next wave
drags her jowls. I see her kind

of joy—it is fast, startled, and
smells sea-worthy this morning.
I cannot see my joy. She runs
south along the waves, drawing

with her the great leash until
it is tearing and I call her name.
The game races back to me. She
tumbles into my legs, catches me

with cold, sandy kiss, soaking
my arms. I say, "Good girl,
good girl." This measure is all
and everything.

Blackberries

The blackberries I eat this morning
have in their flavor road dust,
pollen, and sunlight gathered
and spoke about: sweet
and earthen.

The skin isn't much
to break, a fat warm jewel
pressed to my palate and juiced.
I hold each berry at eye-level

drupelets wicked in fine hairs.
Aggregate seeds multiply in my teeth.
My stained fingers pointing out blue
magna, heart inside some living,
porous and lit. I eat

sunlight's purplish-black answer
to hunger. Light crushing around
my tongue. The night I hid
down in me found to be golden,

after all; a pollinator's domain
when I aim my hand back through
memory and thorns and yellow jackets
for the blackest berries. The bucket I carried
beside my best friend spilling

when we left the road. A momentary coil
knots these places: the berry's constellation
bursting in its brief transit
through ripeness.

I eat the entire carton,
before I leave the farmer's market,
the road the berries grew beside consumed too,
and now I live here, a peace
I've been trying to find all my life.

III.

Reels

Self-Portrait with Teeth

In a wood near Pungo Lake
I untangle juvenile canines
from hair and bone in old scat,
putting their orphaned circle
on my palm. My feral dead
returned by a red wolf, and
I won't leave them again.

A fox maybe. His baby teeth
gnashed enamel fins. I'll ask
a naturalist for the story when
I find the visitor's center.
Right now, the fox is bits
and bob, remnants in my palm

and I don't know which tale
I've wandered in. A poor trade
for magic beans? I have no ax.
All around me water lips
in the cottonwoods. Long-
stemmed mushrooms use

a downed cypress to get above
the marsh. Trumpeter swans
in the first weeks of a winter revival
quartet over my head. Yet here
is gnawing and hunger enough.
I'll trade you your brown cow

for these teeth. Jung said, the gold is
in the shit. Here is why I am alone,
channeling a grave, no longer rank
or wretched, but arranged on my palm.
My shovel and burlap left at home,
but I know what's going down.

At the Presbyterian Hospital

I shake the paper skyline inside a snow globe
stamped *New Mexico*; a coyote slips behind
a cactus on his back and an equally large
rattlesnake weaves down from heaven.

Another lukewarm pool where the trouble
is fixed. The iron center working levers
in the heart machine, guides your
wide mouth back into the waves.

Song for the pale cage, an inescapable,
careful grasping of your fingers. At least
the orchids are purple and cheered
by frilly pink tongues on the side table.

I wash your earlobes and neck with splinters,
leave for hallway coffee and cups of ice.
"I see how you could dream this," I whisper.
Tin under the rain break articulates the mythology.

Pigeons thrum the ledge after a car horn,
wings plucking a momentary night.
The resolve beneath the ribs, a child
grasping four opaque balloons.

I'll treasure the souvenir. Water heaving
the same players at the sky, and we won't drown
in the grit of happiness, as I fold the sheet
under your chin.

What She Means By Empty

She gave up the girls that spring and moved to a carriage house
on Highway 1 near Elk. I was washing a blue mug at her sink
and looking hard at the windowsill, an abalone shell filled
with Monarch Butterflies, their carcasses unchanged
vine and coil of orange and black
offering a petal-wing bouquet.

She welcomed me, sure,
but stepped outside to smoke.
Every ledge was occupied by crystals, driftwood, trinket
boxes—my sisters' milk teeth in a velvet-lined wooden egg.
With a cigarette burning low, she watched the sea
and didn't see me looking.

A window wheezed in the small house
and it was cold. I couldn't stay. I still couldn't forgive her,
though I waited in a chair and felt the sinking
rumble of a truck speeding over a pothole,
and I went back to the butterfly shrine.

Every wing I touched left dust on my fingers
and I felt how it was to destroy a creature
who had spent a long time growing beautiful.
Once you go down there
among the bulbs and the bitches,
you don't get to change your mind.

She stood out there sucking the smoke
while jersey cows pastured next door
put their heads over the fence;
sometimes she gave them handfuls of grass
from her un-trampled yard. I watched.
Every passing car was a speedy disappearance,
a loss to know later.

Take Only Pictures

—Tent Rocks, NM

After the last rain,
                in runnels between rocks,
                        obsidian blinks through
      red and pink crust.

At the other end of the canyon,
                mom leans her camera over Indian Bush,
                        and stops to push blonde
      fly-away under her hat.

Out through the teeth, and eons ago,
                a cleaving of lava, cooled quickly
                        into glass, a continent's birth.
      Today, I know how to maneuver

beyond the "Trail End" sign, even,
                "Warning: Falling Rock" doesn't hold me
                        back. Usually under quartz, the black-eye waits.
      I rub dirt from the opaque luster

and tuck it into my purse. I pull my face
                away from the ground. "This is amazing," I yell
                        into the canyon. She moves toward me now,
      looking out at the mountains. She'll burn;

I worry about her paleness in this way.
                Somehow, she was strong enough to bear
                        my brownness into the world. "We are all
      people of color" and "We don't see color"

–two mantra's assuaging questions
        about race as far back
                as I can remember. At the red earth,
     in these rocks, digging out the eyes,

balm for someone's claim betrayed and
        renamed, I still carry the uncertainty
            of both roots, and they are at war in me.
   "Have you found enough?" she yells.

Back on the trail, I show her a fist of obsidian.
        "Why are they called Apache Tears?" I ask.
          (Honor is loss named.)
   By then we are out of the canyon

and climbing to where she parked the car on the road.
        Sunflowers dip their blazing heads
           over the trail, and every single one of them
   gazes into me.

In Retreat

—Squaw Valley, California

I knew what it meant to stir,
to carry the riddle of tree bark away
from the trunk, to summon fold
upon fold in the press of flight

and push it all against the glass.
I had seen the tribulations before
and won love, like what my mother
held back from my father.

The dream shook in my throat,
its taste waking me. You were
scared I could write so easy, like
I'd slipped on a sheer gown

in the mountains at night. The moth
opened against your lamp light and
stared me down. You were asking
if I'd written the poem before.

I was distant. Then I crossed back
into myself with a laugh that cut
the evening down to frog sounds.
The moth preened its marble head,

the jewel in a tiara you didn't know
you wore. In the dream I traced
stone buttresses along a rocky trail
hiked in the morning. I was up there

when I wrote the poem. The moth
stirred behind you, and I disguised
more laughter with a shallow cough,
until I could write the poem again.

Heron and Night

You are an engine
for these hours, wind turning
into a restlessness having woken
the crescent of a great blue heron

who cackles through song
like a husk torn into, moving over you
all at once, the darkness

in retreat, rushes
to be free of your closeness.
The wings you know
without ever seeing sleep

could be heavy, heaving on Jack's Creek,
as night pulls the seam
away from night, some of it gone

down shore, toward a channel
facing the river.
The piston reed snaps,
the sky torn on the surface

ripples, a splash
returning you to the road,
dismissed and alone.

Everything You Can Burn

With your stick pushing it into embers,
the flag burns out, a stars and stripes offering
in bright blaze, then pithy black scattering

over coals, changing the story, though
you should not burn just anything,
even if it burns itself out—

built-in ignition warnings
and whistle talk. *Hiss*. Spiders crisscross
their climbing into sparks and enter

an ashy ascent, broken away, as a current
must take the shore with it eventually.
A story disguised by flaming doll heads

returns to the mountains, the raft
glances off rocks and men in orange life vests
drop into a whirling torrent. *Pop. Pop.*

You can't stop the tinder of other stars,
amassed as filament, more than breath,
and disappearing through the trees,

or interrupt the teller and dig out
the sap pool before it sizzles awake.
To burn low is to go black,

remember this. And the embers
cleave red birds on the earth; the winged rise,
torn into ravens by the smoke.

Rest Stop

I know while I stretch
the ache through my arms,
that the brown boy jumping
to slap the Exit sign and
the lizard sweeping
his metallic blue tail
across the walk
are not a call
to war.

Between where
and where
his smile peels
open a summer
skin folding us in
cicada song.

Because
youth is a cord
ripped by light
dragging me
into fifteen and
nobody again.
The gymnasium
rocking through
the bleachers
into my bench,
each of us the earth
catches, jammed-up
and crushing.

I am rocked
again. Lungs
splitting, atoms out
the side door, roaring
at the night. Faraway
applause dowsing
brightness for his
journey, that boy
rising up on lightening.

At the Cherry Trees

She eats the cherries all day,
spitting pale pits into her palm.

June's rash of fruit buckled branches
keep her in the shade
where she bites black into red

every time. Jays force their heads
against the cage holes,

bitching at the bounty
housed there. Black,
then all red until the suckled pit

emerges; sweetest around the tart sphere
least changed by sunlight

and never swallowed, though inside
promising infinite Junes,
other girls in the cherry trees.

Black is the night road she cannot see
packed with earth and stars

as each finger leaves her lips. Black
she allows in her wetness
and loves for sticky remnants.

Honey bees mesmerized
by ground rot weave at her legs.

Jays pour a rattling song down
on her. The red held in,
she eats the cherries all day
because she can.

Santa Ana Winds

Much later, after childhood, I understood
her crushing me to the earth
was a hammer's song,
dry and warm around the oaks
and through the grove,
breathing us
into vines of pleasure, lightening
spelling our limbs
into new shoots,
though we named her
different things.

Past tree trunks to the road,
a loosening grip on winter
found your head nodding
wetness in my palm,
a cowlick curling through
my hips. I was a branch her breath
spirited into song, an afternoon
spent in her garments.

And what you had of me:
fingers twisted in my hair,
bow turned to light, gambled
the earth in our cradle

and pulled us both down.
Dresses knotted by knees
and shoes off, elbows turned
to red bark, a fire ant's scorn
blooming behind my ear; she
reached in and we bristled,
swollen and wet,
calling her weather.

Discourse at Lake Champlain

October. Winter already. Snow geese
buffer off shore, a restless ice edge.
We cross the beach and they interrupt
gray sky with white, black under-wing,

a shrill uproar that floods our eardrums
and roots us. By the thousands, their edge
moves deeper on the lake. You're saying,
"if he drowns he cannot rise." As in,

"Look at that drowned man there."
We walk the beach with our backs
to bitter afternoon wind. You teach me
his past: "He tried to drown himself."

"He fell in the lake and drowned."
"She held him under until death occurred."
I press my boot on a white feather
beneath a puddle's glassy eye,

more feathers shifting as I grab them up.
The beach slopes into slate shelves:
rock cut by the water's changing, ends
where the woods come to shore, and

we turn back. The drowned man further
dismissed as your words blow behind us.
The cold pushes our chins to our chests.
The nagging burden of his future

had been there all along, drowning,
drowned, a skin of sand and lake water
disguised by evening.

Always Leaving

Silence rubs out the wind's discourse
eastward. You steer against this, tires
hissing for asphalt. Starlings rush

the Santa Domingo Reservation sign
where horses graze across a red
riverbed. Tumbleweed clears

the highway. White crosses attend
ditches on all sides. Historic routes.
Wreaths shed ribbons and faded

plastic flowers. Wind picks the stuffing
from a teddy bear nailed in place. Problems
cherished at home, bore out as souvenirs,

though you have to reach into the world
from your easiest pocket for the bill.
Stout black junipers wait out the evening,

like boney cattle with their backs to the road.
Light succumbs to the mountains. High beams
demand one narrow path through night.

Manifesto at the Well

You were the blade and the fleck.
You were cut by sunlight
then dropped. What did you

know of water? Not the spine
or the cleft, and February
all the way down. What reason

was there to lean into night? The crinoline dress
of her boredom cinched by ribbons
moved against the light.

A tractor's crumbling work
drifted from the corn field, a faraway opus
moored by crickets.

A fissure of shell, a made-up safety
in the warm palm. She leaned
over the wall, her many brass bangles

clattering around her wrist. You would be
changed, transgressing the space
between here and there.

You expected to always fall.
The only architecture left to a pebble
is stone.

Crown Vetch

Fodder for the goat breaking his lead,
every crown mashed in his cud.
We pulled him from the creek

into a field your mother owned,
mud a brown fleecing he peed
right through while we walked.

We tied him off to a fence
and went for the purple ascent
behind the creek. Your blue jeans

stolen by the fade, you bent over a thick bush
to give me a bouquet that hadn't bloomed,
helmet of green pellets nodding

over your fist. First summer breakage
for girls with their braids fingered-out.
A day soaking in tap water

and the petals melted into frizzy rounds,
sweet houses of tang and musk, littering
pollen inside my bedroom window.

The world was going to be easy
down in the vetch. Isn't it so, isn't it just
the stubbornness of vine,

the strangle growing up the trees
and rooting out all the good it did me
to bring the bouquet home.

Another Crossing

Swallows torque their bodies to fit the rafters,
adapting to blue gaps where the farmer has storied

the night with hay bales. I look from darkness into
the noon hour; crickets scald heat-weary summer

above an earth subdued by alfalfa fields. I lean my hands
over my eyes as your door slams, the windshield's glare

blanking out grief. Mardi Gras beads twist on the
rearview mirror in time with the lurch and choke of gears.

Jade shoots offer heavy-headed praise under the windmill
and my hands fill with dirt and broken rock, the same

as what shatters on the driveway behind your Civic.
A cord snaps between us, lit ends snaking back into the belly
until it kicks me, hard like I'll never swallow.

Thrown

Those hours when
she goes home grazing and
dust she leaves me in,

down some logging road, settles
in my sweat and clothes. I know
I'll never be rid of anger no

matter how many miles we finish
under her hooves. I walk on back,
breath knocked out, horsefly trying

to get in good on a shoulder blade.
I mutter curses: please blister, keep
the burn down. I smell like a horse,

too. Done damage in my mind that
copulates like rabbits in a good year.
Most people don't appreciate

stubborn. Dad called it hard-headedness.
Then I turn down the driveway
and can't whip her or begrudge her

the tireless grasses outside the fence.
I get an apple and taunt her until the
hackamore's strong rein is back

in my grasp, defeated as we walk
side by side to her water trough;
dirty fingers digging in the mane

behind her ears, all the forgiveness
I'd stored up—hers now.

A Wild Thing

If you thought there was sorrow in the bear,
its one-eyed gaze from inside her teeth,
shook against her jowls, and slobbered upon.

If you thought there was a better day
and more fun to be had, the bow
glued at its throat gone, the plaid
vest new with fringe.

Stolen from its shelf where dolls
and stuffed horses waited for parties
and a child's snug sleep to bloom
from its faux fur these clouds.

If you thought to pick polyester fiberfill
out of sunflowers, gather synthetic streamers
across the lawn and caught in the fence spikes
could wear you down.

Your house pulled open by this joy
and the brown dog dancing her flaccid kill
over the gate. So you tug the teddy bear
from her mouth and scold a story
that has put the sky on the earth again.

Here, saying, open that ragged gut of fluff,
be gone in wild places, be grateful anyway
if this is the worst thing that happens
on your street today.

Bodega Head, December

At the absolute edge: waves
claw at the rocks, roaring.
Wind caught in my hood,

roaring. A trail moves us
west so we can look down
into the sea and not fall to

the lowest floor of greening.
Who among us does not wish
to be thrown at the sea? Sun-

light cuts glass in every motion,
roaring. Blackbirds stopped
on a wood fence turn yellow eyes

east. Then they fly or they fall
down cliffs into ruby-tipped
ice plants. On an outcrop,

a man photographs the churning.
In this way we understand
the rocks. The neon

greening beneath the precipice
at the lowest floor. Here is
my photo, looking westward

in the claw light. Waves
born over rocks, roar.

Biographical Note

Amber Flora Thomas is the author of *Eye of Water: Poems*, selected by Harryette Mullen as the winner of the 2004 Cave Canem Poetry Prize, and *The Rabbits Could Sing: Poems*, selected by Peggy Shumaker for the Alaska Literary Series in 2011. A recipient of the Dylan Thomas American Poet Prize, Richard Peterson Prize, and Ann Stanford Prize, her poetry has appeared in *Callaloo, Orion Magazine, Alaska Quarterly Review, Saranac Review*, and *Crab Orchard Review*, as well as *Angles of Ascent: A Norton Anthology of Contemporary African American Poetry* and numerous other journals and anthologies. She is a Cave Canem Fellow and faculty member. She received her MFA from Washington University in St. Louis in 1998. She was born and raised in Northern California. Currently, she is an Associate Professor of Creative Writing at East Carolina University.